W9-DAE-917

Mississippi
The Magnolia State

Miriam Coleman

PowerKiDS press™

New York

Published in 2011 by The Rosen Publishing Group, Inc.
29 East 21st Street, New York, NY 10010

First Edition

Editor: Joanne Randolph
Book Design: Greg Tucker
Layout Design: Kate Laczynski
Photo Researcher: Jessica Gerweck

Photo Credits: Cover, p. 1 © Bill Barksdale/age fotostock; p. 5 Anne Rippy/Getty Images; p. 7 Buyenlarge/Getty Images; p. 9 © Nedra Westwater/age fotostock; pp. 11, 19 © Dennis MacDonald/age fotostock; p. 13 © Colin Jones/age fotostock; p. 15 © www.istockphoto.com/Lev Radin; p. 17 Ira Block/Getty Images; p. 22 (tree) © www.istockphoto.com/Pavel Cheiko; p. 22 (deer, mockingbird, honeybee) Shutterstock.com; p. 22 (Wells-Barnett) R. Gates/Hulton Archive/Getty Images; p. 22 (Faulkner) STF/AFP/Getty Images; p. 22 (Presley) Michael Ochs Archives/Getty Images.

Library of Congress Cataloging-in-Publication Data

Coleman, Miriam.
  Mississippi : the Magnolia State / Miriam Coleman. — 1st ed.
      p. cm. — (Our amazing states)
  Includes index.
  ISBN 978-1-4488-0653-9 (library binding) — ISBN 978-1-4488-0738-3 (pbk.) — ISBN 978-1-4488-0739-0 (6-pack)
  1. Mississippi—Juvenile literature. I. Title.
  F341.3.C65 2011
  976.2—dc22
                                                2009052013

Manufactured in the United States of America

CPSIA Compliance Information: Batch #WS10PK: For Further Information contact Rosen Publishing, New York, New York at 1-800-237-9932

Contents

Welcome to Mississippi

Mississippi is a state in the southern part of the United States. The name Mississippi means "father of the waters" in the language of the people who lived there thousands of years ago. The state is named after the great Mississippi River, which flows along its western border. This part of the state is good for farming.

In northwest Mississippi, the river flooded its banks for many years. It made the soil rich and dark. This area is called the Mississippi Delta. This one small part of the country is also famous for a style of music called the Delta **blues**. The blues had a large influence on jazz and early rock and roll.

A riverboat floats on the Mississippi River in Natchez, Mississippi, shown here. Natchez was the first lasting settlement on the Mississippi River.

Cotton Fields and Battlefields

The first people came to Mississippi around 12,000 years ago. Among the Native Americans who lived there were the Chickasaw, Choctaw, Natchez, and Biloxi tribes. In the 1600s, French settlers came to farm the good soil. They brought enslaved people from Africa to work the fields.

On December 10, 1817, Mississippi became the twentieth state of the **Union**. By this time, Mississippi was rich with cotton **plantations** worked by slaves. When the **Civil War** began in 1861, Mississippi did not want slavery to end. It was the second state to **secede** from the Union. After many battles, the **Confederate** States, including Mississippi, lost the war and rejoined the Union.

In 1863, the Confederate army fought the Union army in Vicksburg, Mississippi, for 47 days. The Union gained control of the whole Mississippi River in this battle.

Historic Beauvoir

If you are interested in Confederate history, you could visit Beauvoir, in Biloxi, Mississippi. This plantation house was the last home of Confederate president Jefferson Davis. He moved into the house in 1877.

When Davis died, his widow sold the house to the Sons of Confederate Veterans. She wanted veterans and widows of the Confederacy to live in the house at no cost. It was used for this purpose from 1903 until 1957.

She also asked that the house be used as a memorial to Jefferson Davis and the Confederate soldier. Today, visitors can tour the home and the Jefferson Davis Presidential Library and Museum.

You can learn about Jefferson Davis's life, his time as president of the Confederacy, and about the Civil War from the Confederate point of view at Beauvoir.

A Road Through Time

The Natchez Trace Parkway is an ancient road that runs from Nashville, Tennessee, to Natchez, Mississippi. It is 444 miles (715 km) long, and more than 300 miles (483 km) of it are in Mississippi.

The first people to travel along this path were the Natchez, Choctaw, and Chickasaw Native Americans. Later, **pioneers** used the trail as they **explored** the land along the Mississippi River.

Today, the Natchez Trace Parkway is sometimes called a ribbon of time because it allows travelers to see so many important spots in Mississippi's history. It takes you past grand old plantation houses, ancient Native American villages, and the battlefield of Vicksburg.

This boardwalk lets visitors explore a cypress swamp along the Natchez Trace Parkway. There is a lot to see on the trace!

The Land of Mississippi

There are two main land areas in Mississippi. The rich land of the Mississippi Alluvial Plain, also called the Mississippi Delta, makes up the western part of the state, near the Mississippi River. The East Gulf Coastal Plain, in the eastern part of the state, has many low hills and forests. Woodall Mountain, in the Tennessee River Hills of northeastern Mississippi, is the highest point in the state, at 804 feet (245 m). The southeast edge of Mississippi is on the Gulf of Mexico.

Mississippi's summers are hot with lots of rain and thunderstorms. The winters are short and mostly mild.

This is the Mississippi Delta. The land in this area near the river has lots of water in between pieces of land because the river has been dropping off bits of land over time.

Magnolias and More

Mississippi is a land of trees. More than half of Mississippi is covered in forest. Cottonwood, hickory, oak, and pine trees all grow in Mississippi. Mississippi's most famous tree is the magnolia. In fact, it is the official state tree. Magnolias are evergreen trees that have large flowers in the spring. They grow all over Mississippi and give it its nickname, the Magnolia State.

Many different animals live in Mississippi's forests and in its streams, rivers, and fields, too. Beavers, deer, foxes, ducks, turkeys, and catfish all make a home in Mississippi. Mockingbirds delight listeners with their singing throughout the state. The mockingbird became the state bird in 1941.

Magnolias often have white flowers but can grow in other colors, too. Their leaves are thick, shiny, and green.

What Mississippi Makes

About one-third of Mississippi is farmland. Mississippi farmers grow huge amounts of cotton, pecans, peaches, and watermelons. Mississippi farms raise much of the chicken and cattle that the rest of the country eats, too. Mississippi is also the catfish capital of the world! The town of Belzoni holds a **festival** every year to **celebrate** this tasty fish.

Mississippi is also an important place for shipping. The Mississippi River goes all the way north to Minnesota and connects Mississippi river port cities, like Greenville and Natchez, to the rest of the country. Gulfport and Pascagoula have seaports where ships come in from all around the world. Pascagoula also has busy shipyards where those ships are built.

Here a farmworker packs cotton onto a truck during the cotton harvest. Mississippi cotton farmers make and sell around $598 million in cotton each year.

We're Going to Jackson!

Jackson became Mississippi's capital city in 1821. Named after President Andrew Jackson, the city lies along the Pearl River. Jackson has more people living in it than any other city in Mississippi.

Like most of Mississippi, Jackson was a hard place for African Americans through most of its history. They were treated badly and segregated, or forced to live separately, from white people. In the 1960s, as part of the **civil rights movement**, many people came to Jackson to stop this bad treatment. A group called the Freedom Riders rode buses into Jackson to **protest** against segregation. The struggle of the brave people who spoke up in Jackson led to great changes all over the South.

Mississippi's capitol was built in 1903 and is 180 feet (55 m) tall at the top of its dome. This is the third capitol that has been used in Jackson.

Visiting the Magnolia State

People come from all over the world to enjoy Mississippi's natural beauty, from the Piney Woods to the sunny Gulf Coast beaches. The Mississippi Petrified Forest is a beautiful place to explore, too. Mississippi is also a great place to learn about history up close. You can see battlefields such as Vicksburg and Tupelo and learn about the terrible costs of the Civil War. You can visit grand old plantation houses to see how wealthy people once lived in the old South.

At the Delta Blues Museum in Clarksdale, you can learn all about Mississippi musicians, such as Robert Johnson and B. B. King. There are so many ways to celebrate the **culture** that grew from the rich soil of this amazing state!

Glossary

blues (BLOOZ) Sad songs that came from songs used to honor God.

celebrate (SEH-leh-brayt) To observe an important occasion with special activities.

civil rights movement (SIH-vul RYTS MOOV-mint) People and groups working together to win freedom and equality for all.

Civil War (SIH-vul WOR) The war fought between the Northern and the Southern states of America from 1861 to 1865.

Confederate (kun-FEH-duh-ret) Part of a group of 11 Southern states that announced themselves separate from the United States in 1860 until 1865.

culture (KUL-chur) The beliefs, practices, and arts of a group of people.

explored (ek-SPLORD) Traveled and looked for new land.

festival (FES-tih-vul) A day or special time of parties and feasting.

pioneers (py-uh-NEERZ) Some of the first people to settle in a new area.

plantations (plan-TAY-shunz) Very large farms where crops are grown.

protest (proh-TEST) To act in disagreement of something.

secede (sih-SEED) To withdraw from a group or a country.

Union (YOON-yun) Another name for the United States that refers to the joining, or uniting, of the various states into one nation.

Mississippi State Symbols

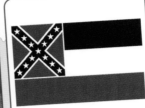

State Tree
Magnolia

State Land Mammal
White-Tailed Deer

State Flag

State Bird
Mockingbird

State Insect
Honeybee

State Seal

Famous People from Mississippi

Ida B. Wells-Barnett
(1862–1931)
Born in Holy Springs, MS
Journalist/Civil
Rights and Women's
Rights Leader

William Faulkner
(1897–1962)
Born in New Albany, MS
Author

Elvis Presley
(1935–1977)
Born in Tupelo, MS
Singer and Musician

Mississippi State Map

Corinth

Woodall Mountain

Sardis Lake

Tupelo

Grenada Lake

Mississippi Delta

Greenville

Big Black River

Pearl River

Yazoo City

Yazoo River

Ross Barnett Resevoir

Meridian

★ Jackson

Mississippi River

Natchez

Hattiesburg

Gulfport

Biloxi

Gulf of Mexico

Legend

○ Major City

★ Capital

〜 River

Mississippi State Facts

Population: About 2,844,638

Area: 47,695 square miles (123,529 sq km)

Motto: "Virtute et Armis" (By Valor and Arms)

Song: "Go Mississippi," by Houston Davis

Index

Web Sites

Due to the changing nature of Internet links, PowerKids Press has developed an online list of Web sites related to the subject of this book. This site is updated regularly. Please use this link to access the list:

www.powerkidslinks.com/amst/ms/